i love it when i can walk into a building and look up to discover a new galaxy. so many worlds, scattered throughout the big cities — rewards for the artists and religious. this planet, i named DARQUAVIOUS FUNKMASTER JIGGY THE THIRD.

found DARQUAVIOUS FUNKMASTER JIGGY THE THIRD in chicago, accompanying a friend tryna reunite with their crush.

105mm ⋄ f/8 ⋄ 1/60   2020

coronavirus at corona plaza;
the world was turning to ruin as our
infected grubby little fingers played
chess on the subway.

55mm ◇ f/4 ◇ 1/80   2021

It all calls back.

We experience something now, remember it later, and more likely than not—we forget it eventually. Memories sprout from so many collided moments, and they stay as long as they need. Aging, disease, trauma, etc. can all effect how vividly we remember the life we've lived. I think a photograph can bring a sense of reverence to what would otherwise fade easily to the life around us. Each one is a seed, a planted moment, capable of extending deep roots—ready to grow memories we'll only grow fonder for.

Here, you'll find some of mine :^)

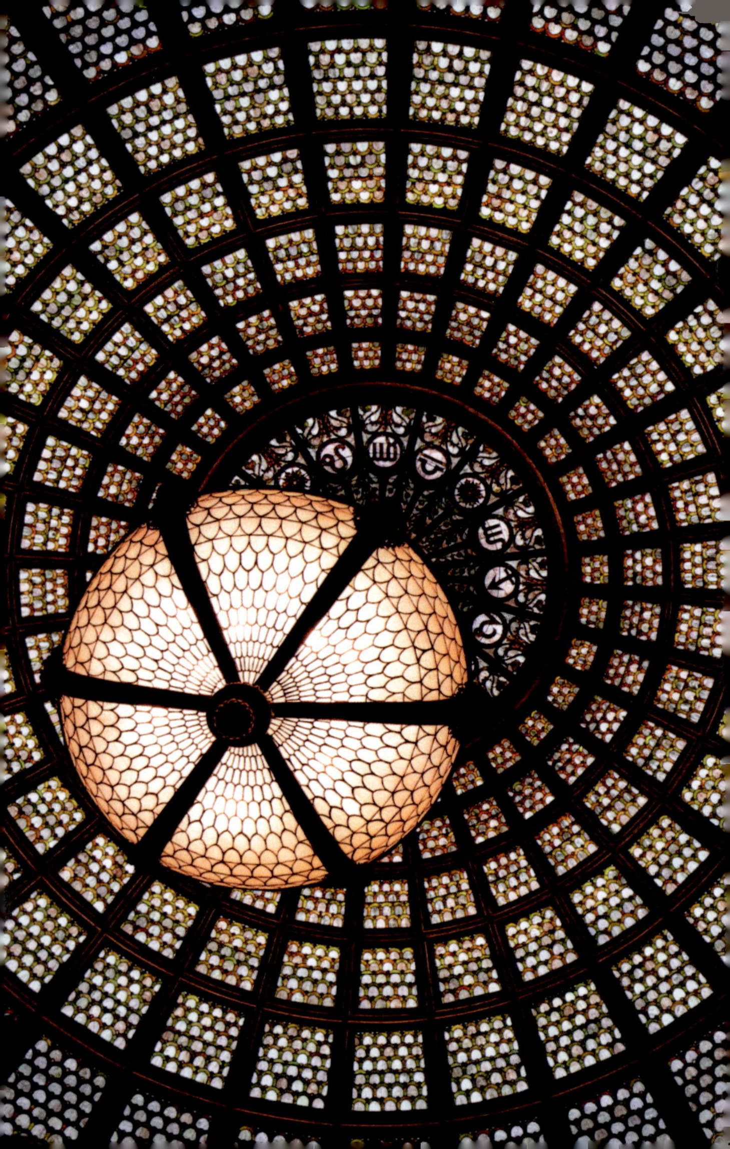

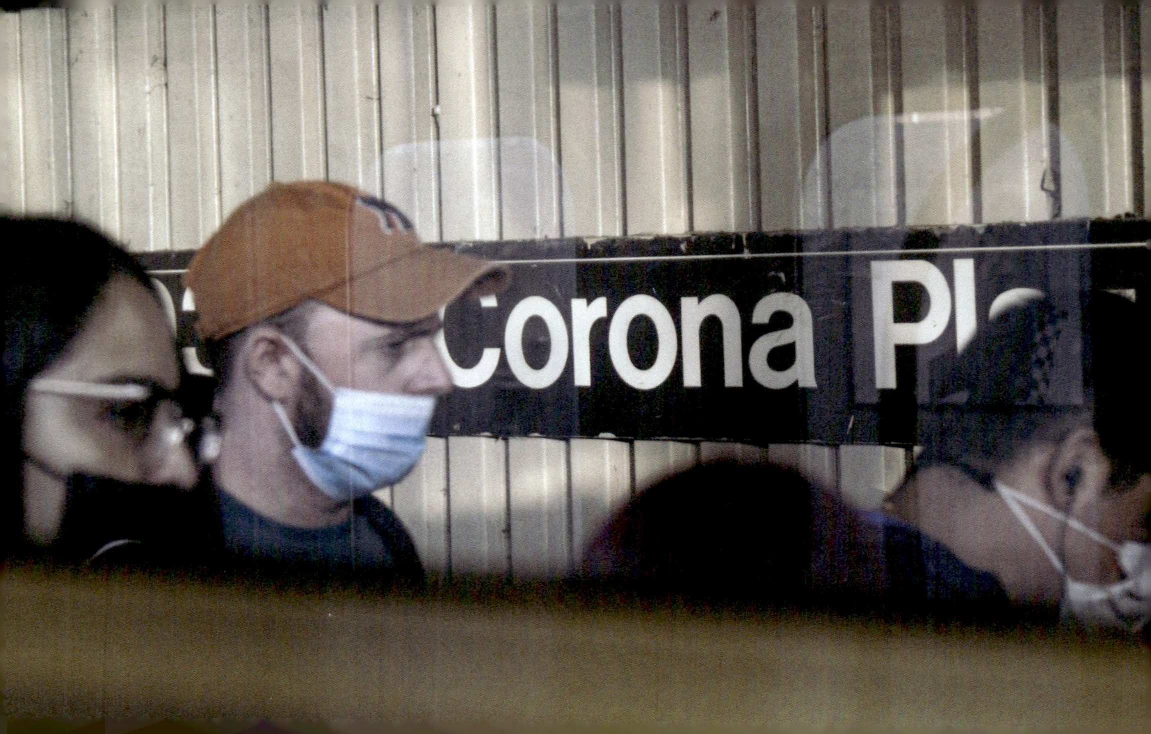
Corona Pl

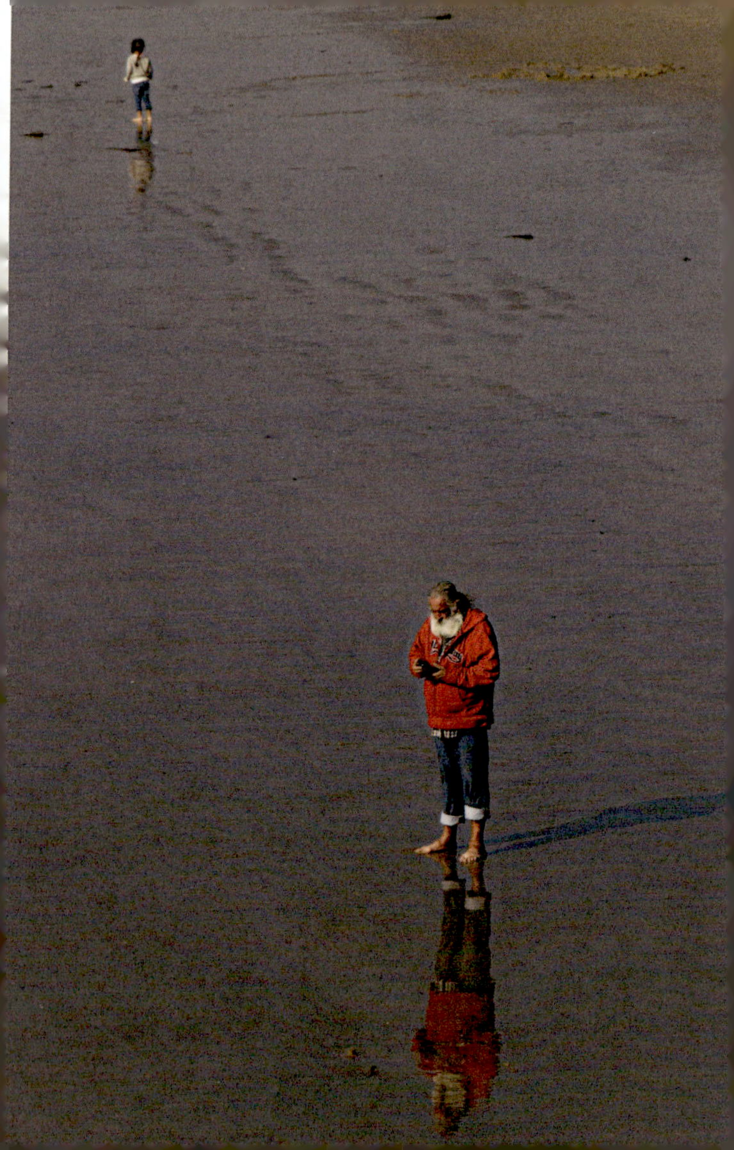

found santa and his elf at
santa monica — they really
thought they was slick;
think about it, who would
want to spend summer at
the north pole??? exactly.

75mm ◇ f/11 ◇ 1/400   2019

monterey, roadtrippin and
helping a friend make a film.
as they directed, we just
floated around to their
whim — sparing the details.
and just being a part of what
we knew was gonna be
beautiful.

28mm ◇ f/2.8 ◇ 1/50   2025

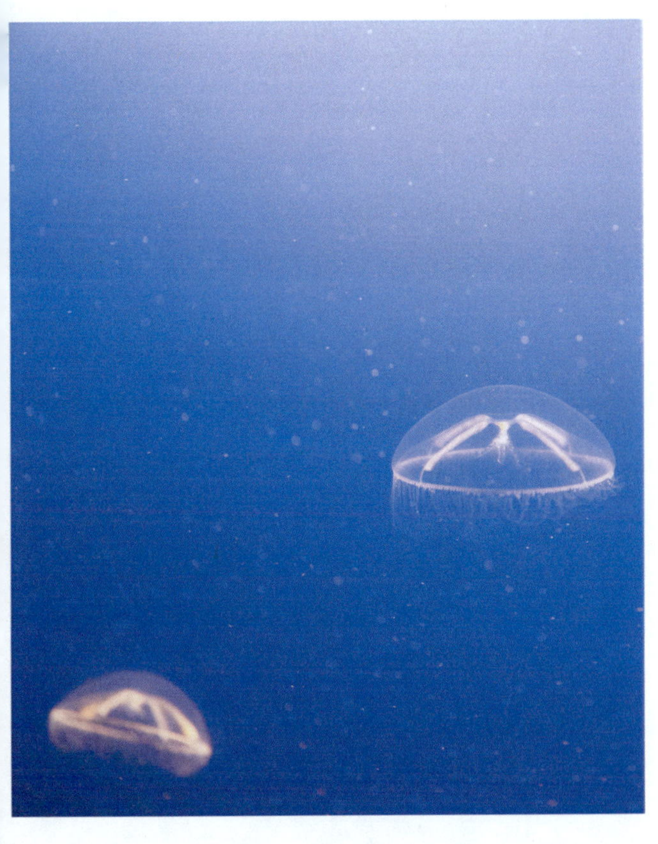

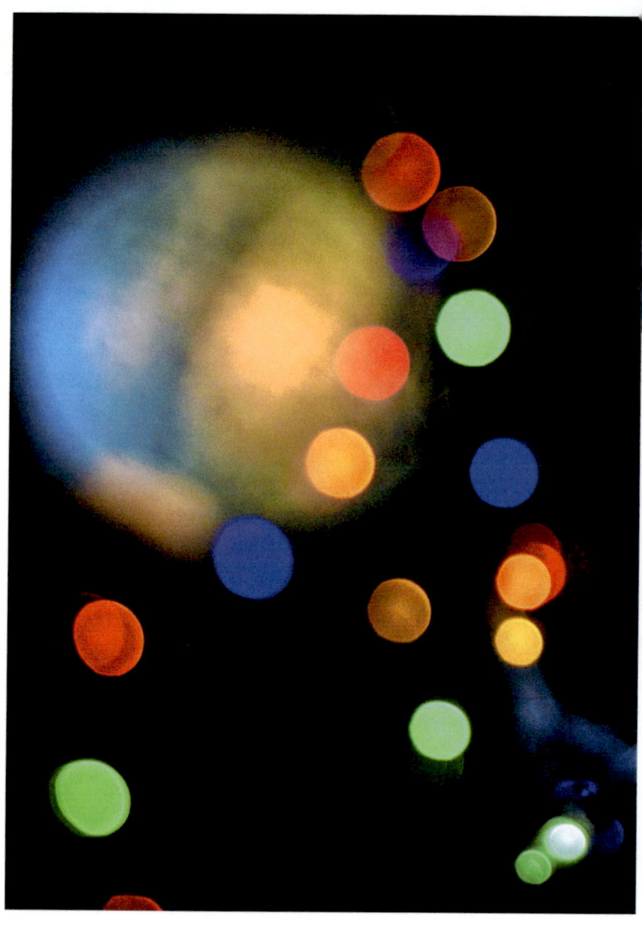

28mm ✧ f/2.8 ✧ 1/200   2019

stardust video and coffee. you gave me a home. one dollar coffee, five dollar tots, moody baristas, tattooed bathrooms, curated playlists, warm window nooks. i would spend fourteen hours a day with you, and i never felt like i was intruding. it was come as you are, grow as you are. your people encouraged my interviews, photoshoots, writing binges. you calmed my nerves when meeting new people. provided a stage to musicians who had never stepped foot onto one. you gave sanctuary to the homeless. solace to the lonely. refuge for the creative. for every seven dollars i made per hour, six were happily saved for you.

with love,
azeem

this group was so cute. just
a couple of fellas bikin
under the moonlight. when
they passed, i was greeted
with big ol' smiles as they
climbed higher and higher
closer to that disc in the sky.

105mm ◇ f/2.8 ◇ 1/60   2024

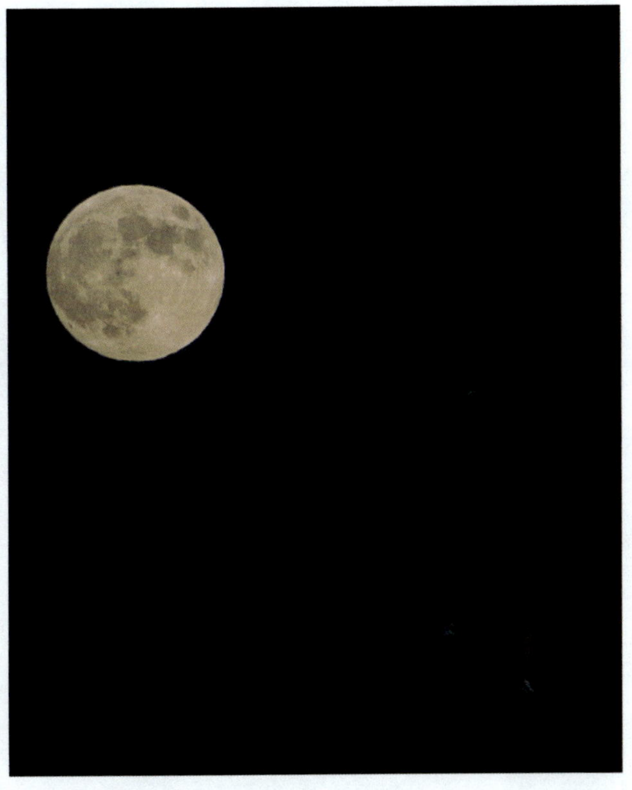

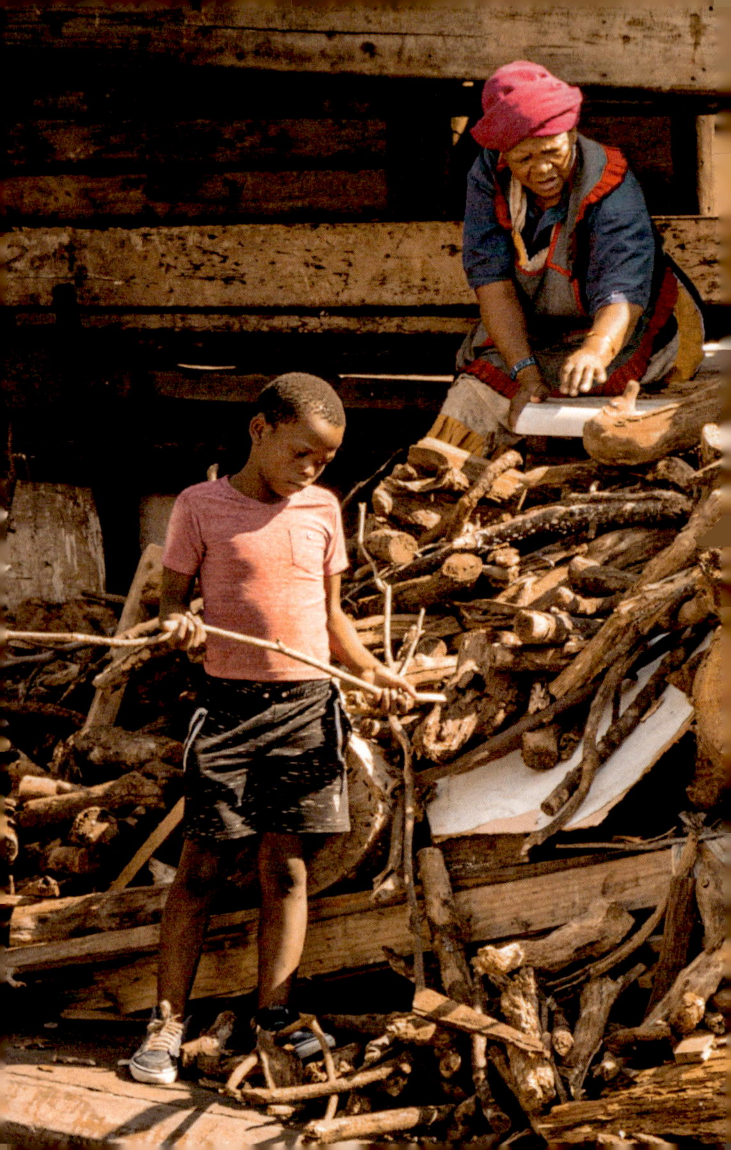

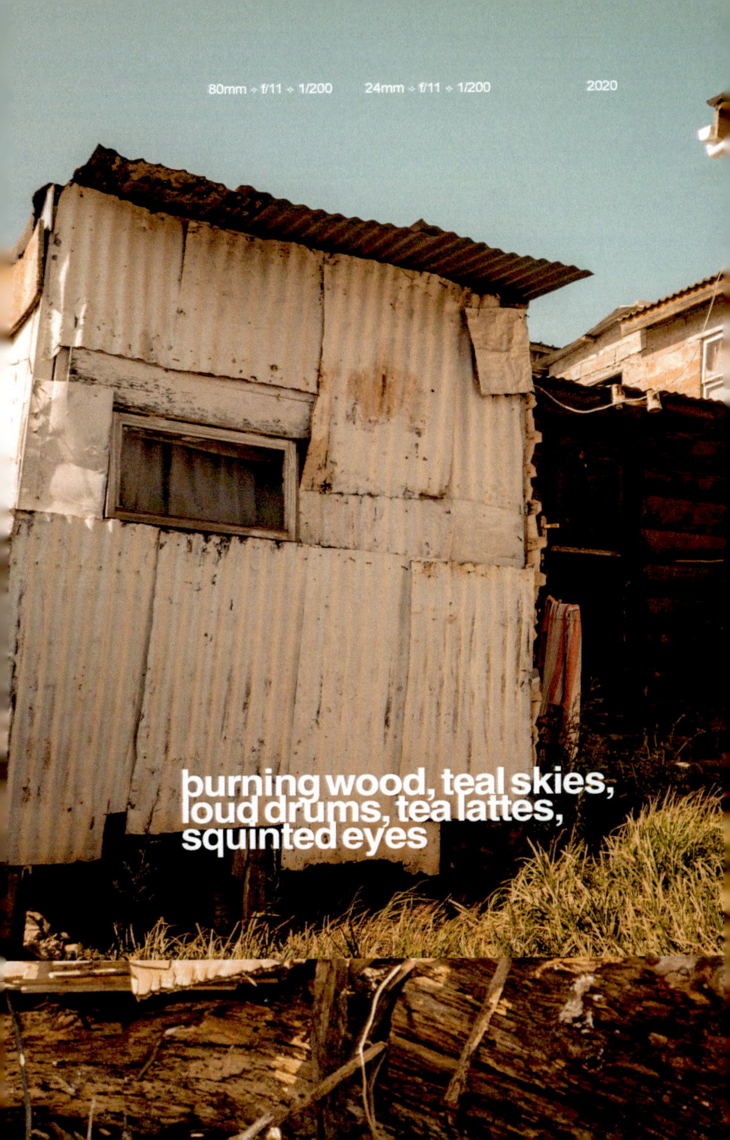
80mm ✧ f/11 ✧ 1/200   24mm ✧ f/11 ✧ 1/200   2020
burning wood, teal skies,
loud drums, tea lattes,
squinted eyes

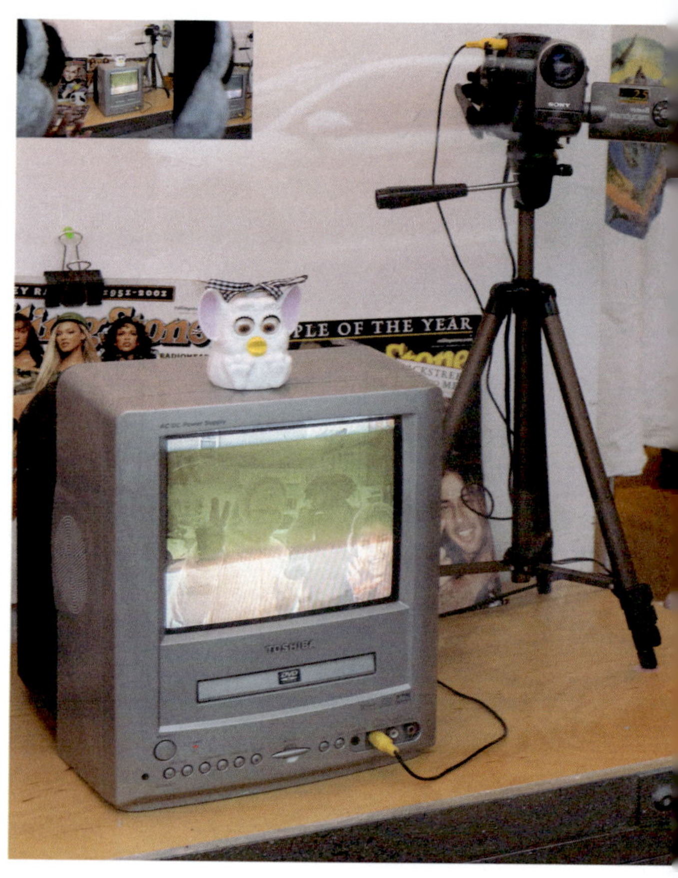

had the most banger eggs
and potatoes this day and
i don't even like eggs but
idk it just hit. went to
some thrifts, stared at
some books, made new
connections with both
old and new people.

at some point... we
realized we were being
watched......... but it's chill!
it was cool! furby!

28mm ⋄ f/5 ⋄ 1/125   2025

shoutout to the bird people.
they be talkin to the birds and
i swear the birds be
responding back. It's a
special flavor of community
and I like to believe the
connection's mutual, no
animal — human or winged —
will approach unless there's
a level of comfort. And sure,
yeah, there's food
incentive — but I feel like a
warm meal could do the
same for us.

45mm ◇ f/11 ◇ 1/320   2019

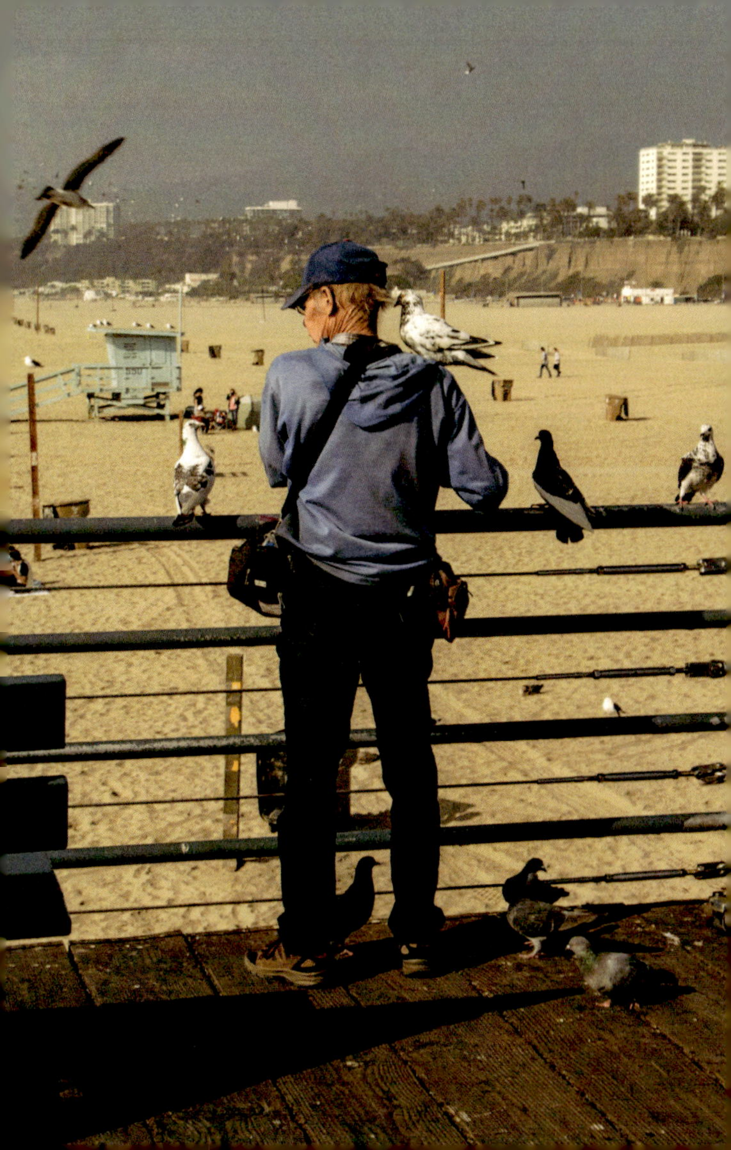

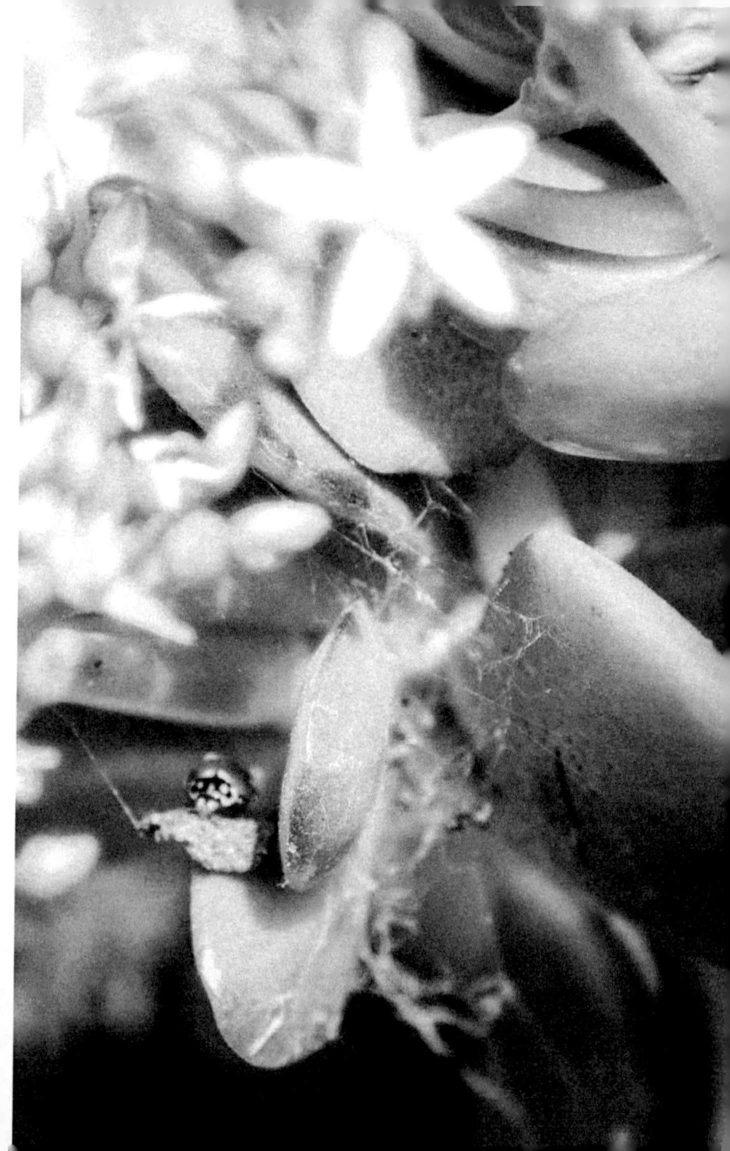

i wonder if this ladybug
knew of the lil situation it was
in.. surround by legions of
spiderwebs under a star. i
found it beautiful but i doubt
the mosquito caught right
next to her liked it very much .
yeah.. hakuna matata?

105mm ✧ f/4 ✧ 1/160   2017

as a fan of both La La Land and
The Prince of Tennis, this was a
delightful intersection. Catch me
rehearsing the choreography of
Planetarium at the Griffith
Observatory then practicing my
forehand all on a crisp
wednesday afternoon. It's
gonna happen, it has to happen.

drove up here after delivering
break-up clothes to my ex;
kendrick dropped not like us;
saw another ryan gosling movie
at the chinese theatre — blandest
popcorn I've ever had in my life it
was like they sucked all the high
blood pressure out of it

47mm ⋄ f/11 ⋄ 1/200   2024

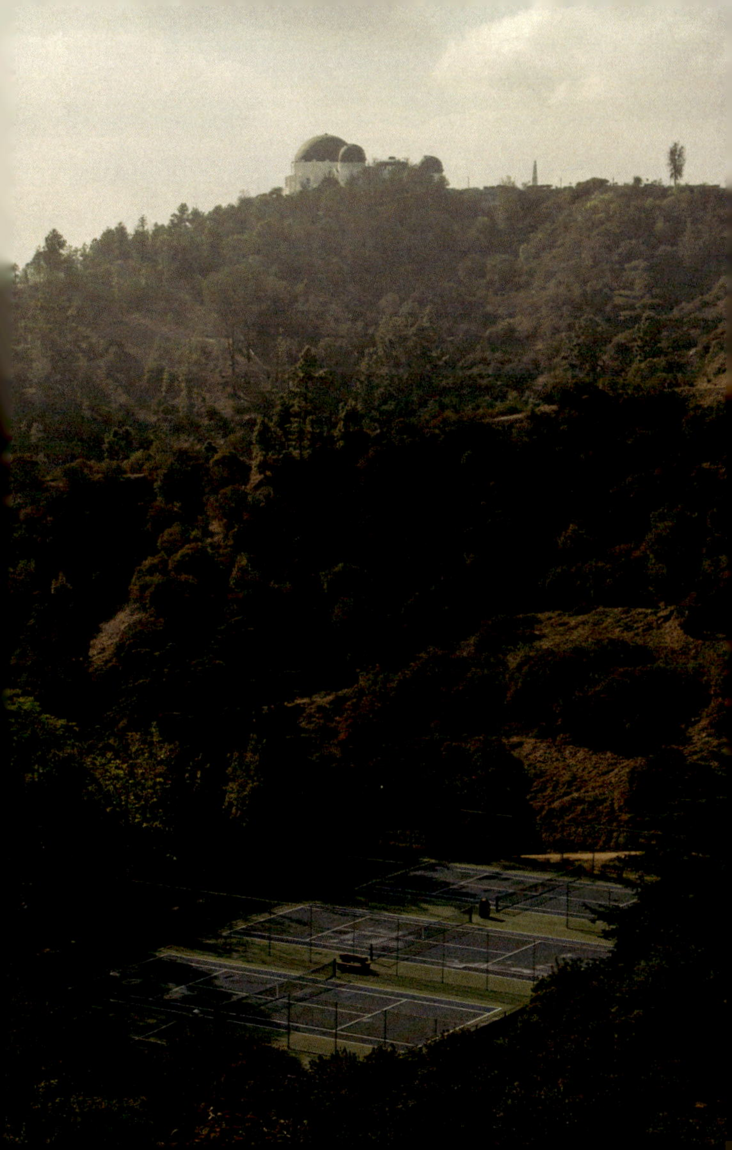

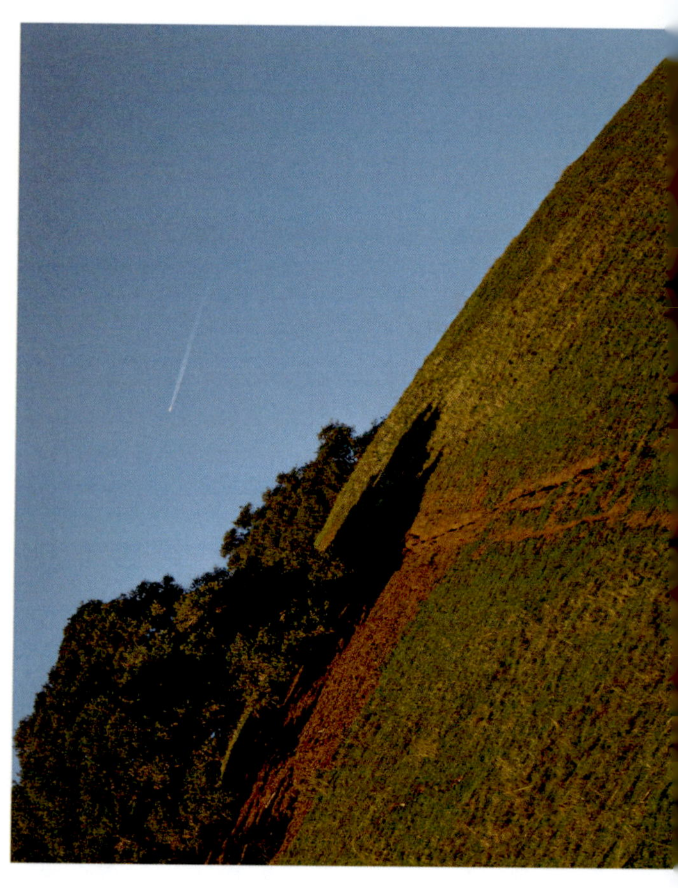

another day at garin regional.
this place holds such a
valuable spot in my heart. in
the few days after just
moving to california, it
brought me comfort in this
new land. the sky is always
so clear and the hills be rollin,
so time starts to become
irrelevant. Sometimes I'd just
walk and just keep on walkin

28mm ✧ f/16 ✧ 1/125   2023

seattle, conversations
with a dear friend about
work, passions,
pressures, and enjoying
life while black. he
showed me a new park,
and we ate ice cream on
the grass.

5mm ✧ f/3.2 ✧ 1/800   2023

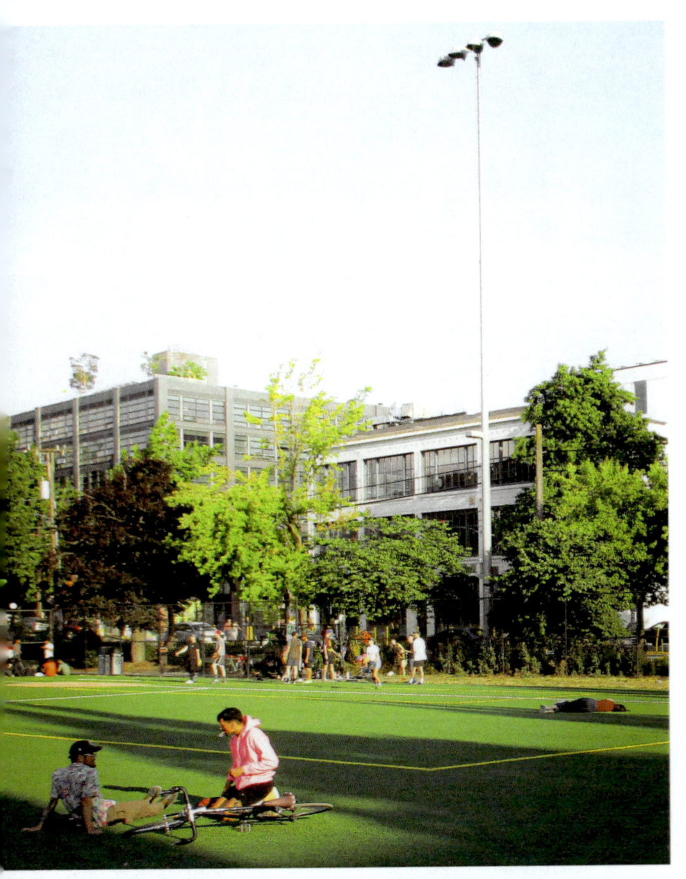

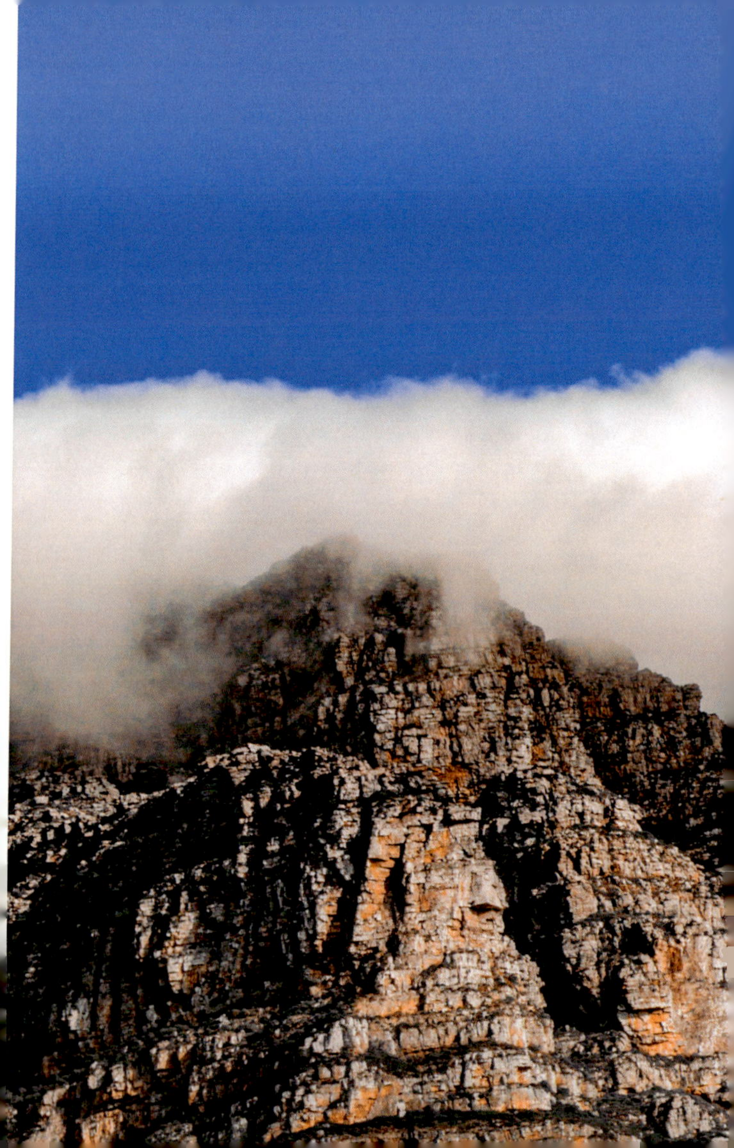

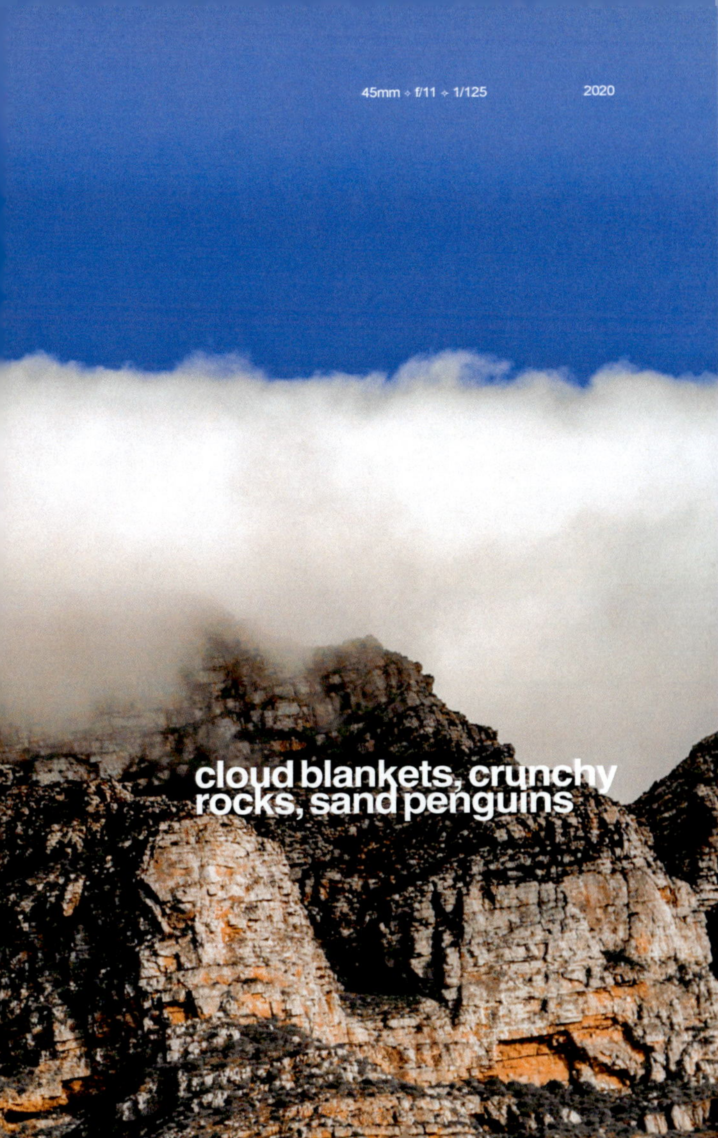
45mm ÷ f/11 ÷ 1/125   2020
cloud blankets, crunchy
rocks, sand penguins

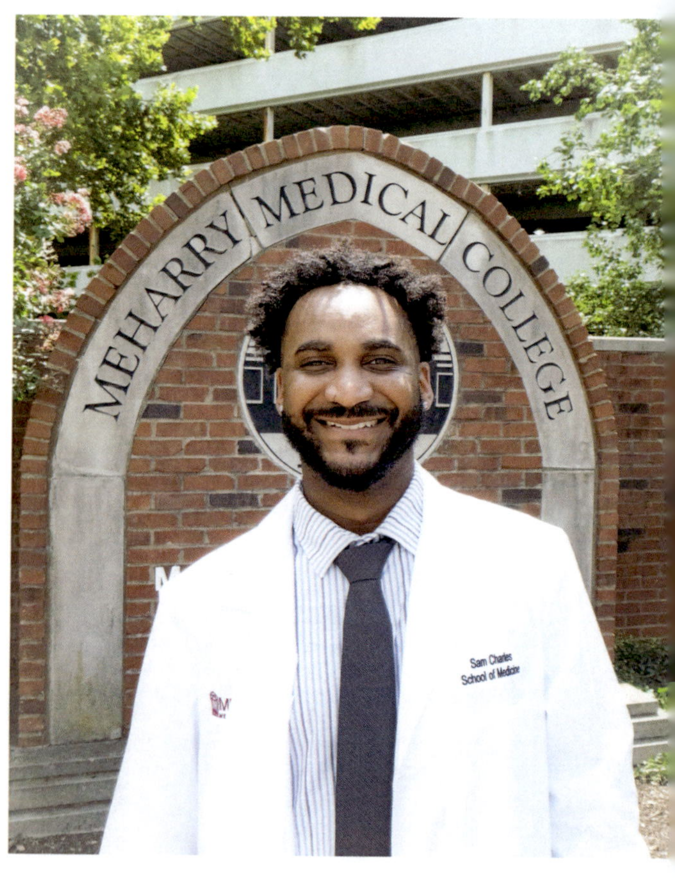
MEHARRY MEDICAL COLLEGE
Sam Charles
School of Medicine

this is sam. i've see sam hit so
many walls to attaining his
dream, and in this moment i
was able to capture him
stepping right over one. i'm
so proud of him, and this
photo gives me the widest
smile. he still ugly tho

7mm ✦ f/4 ✦ 1/600   2025

CUE SCARY MUSIC

she was about to eat me.

wandering this museum, watching my back at every turn. I i thought i was careful, but alas, past the old pottery in glass cases, i see her — gazing ravenously, ready to strike. alas! this cannibal was caught in the act, and i live to tell the tale. we got pho after

28mm ◇ f/2.8 ◇ 1/125   2025

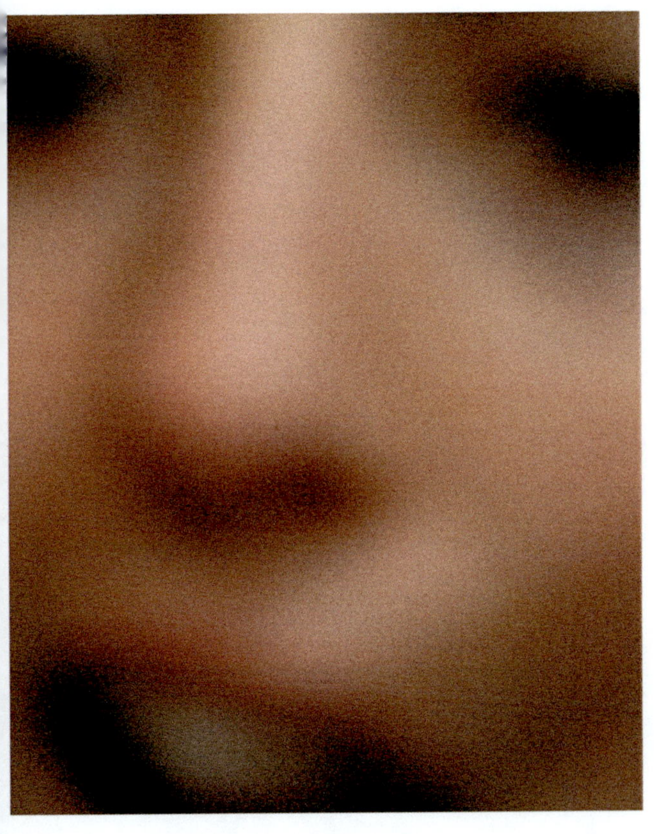

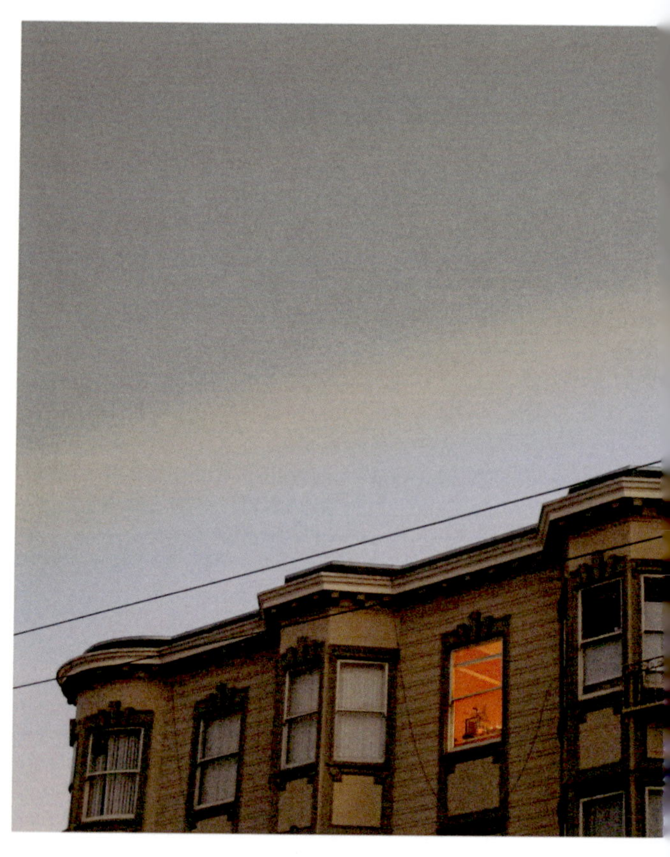

another window to add to the
catalogue. i feel like they say so
much about a person's
lifestyle. gazing upwards in san
francisco, windows will reveal
every flag under the sun,
thousand year-old pothos, and
the mightiest of surveilence
cats. this window in little italy is
always **radiating orange** amidst
the protective blinds
surrounding it. every time i'm
out there, even on the foggiest
days, it's lighting up the sky. i
wonder what kind of life this
person lives..

35mm ⋄ f/8 ⋄ 1/80   2023

I've never seen a man so
excited to ride a bike. I said
"yeah you should take it for
a spin!" man disappeared.

thankfully, he comes back
around — gleefully dashing
down the train tracks of
west oakland, inhibited by
no one.

SX-70 125 ISO round ⋄ sonar focused   2025

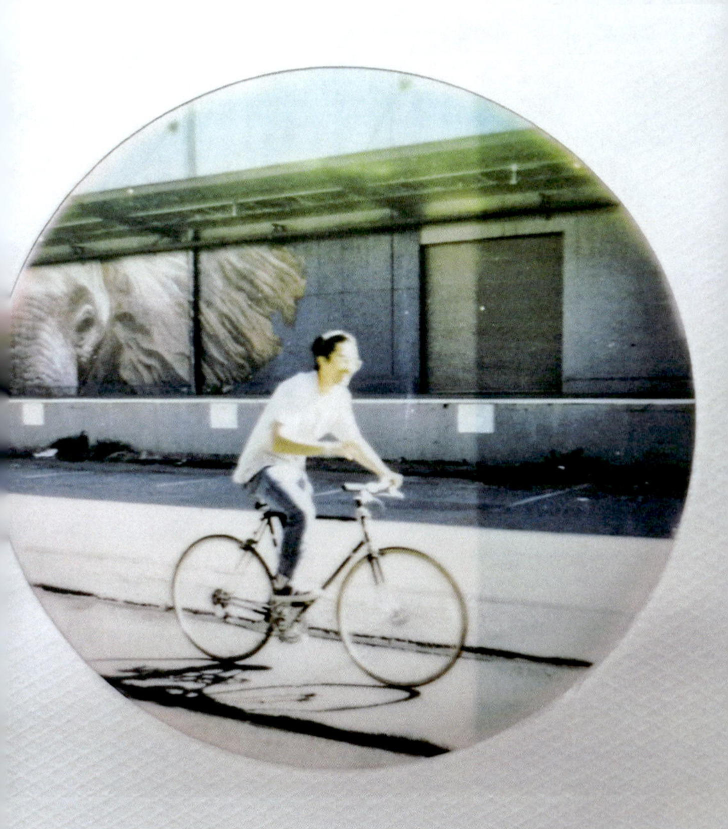

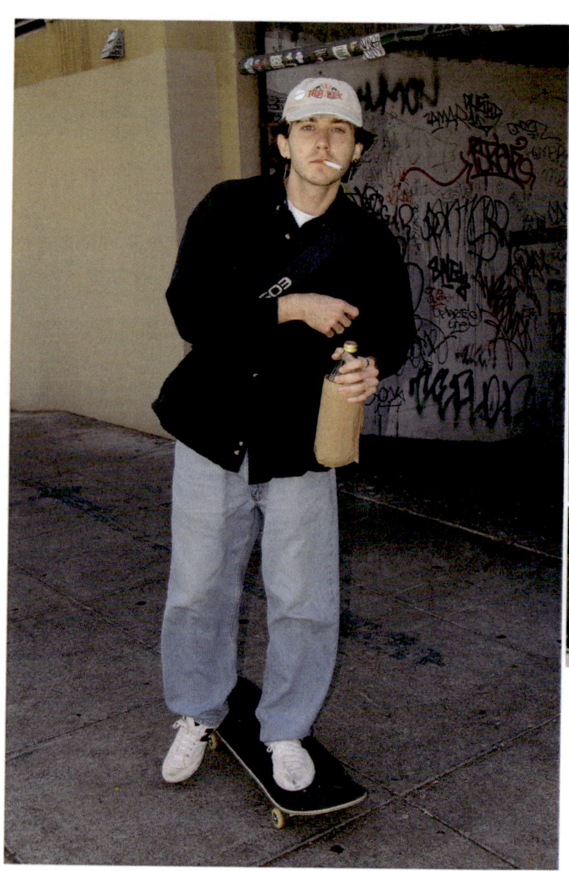

international skate day in sf.
full of wheels , people with an
aptitude for falling, and where
i'd expect water to be in hand,
it'd be a forty in a paper bag. i
had just learned how to
halfhazardly do something
only some would consider an
ollie. was able to blend in by
channeling my inner tony .

28mm ◇ f/4 ◇ 1/200   28mm ◇ f/4 ◇ 1/1000   2025

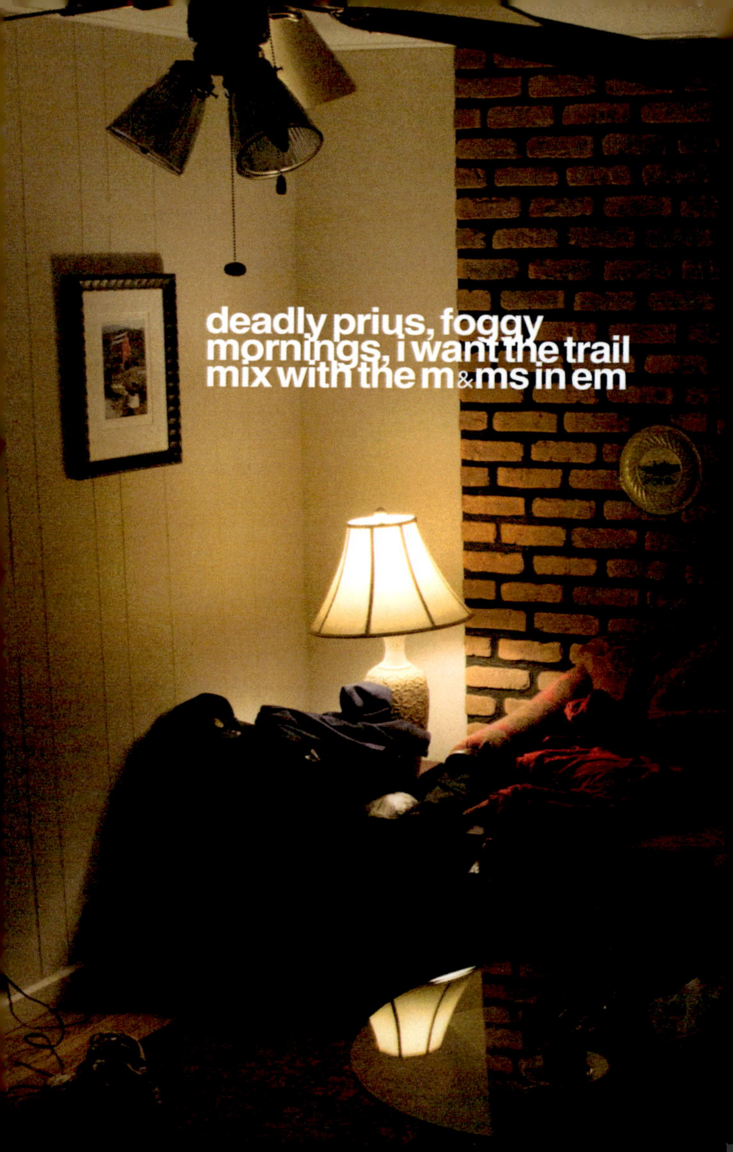

deadly prius, foggy mornings, i want the trail mix with the m&ms in em

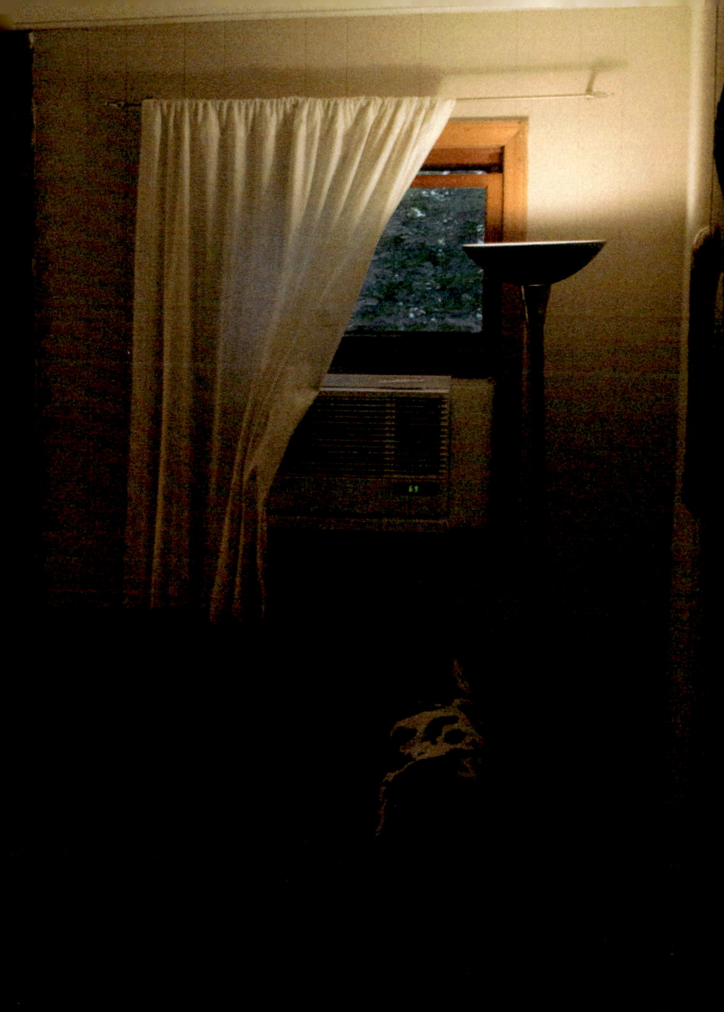

24mm ◇ f/8 ◇ 1/80
2019

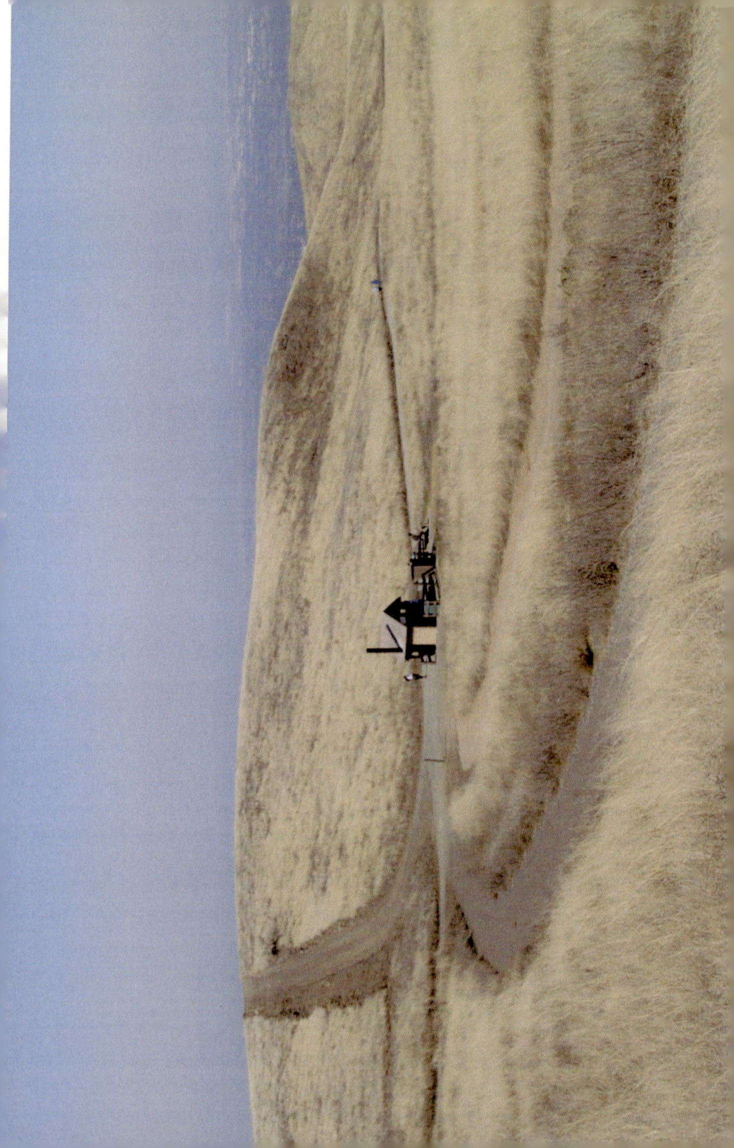

it's moments like this that makes it so hard for me to believe in the mundane. like you're telling me i can just walk outside and end up in wizard of oz? the magic is undeniable when we wonder just how strange the world is. fill a strange world with billions of unique lives and we get this straight up mystical bathroom. i didn't get to go in but i'm sure there's fireflies or somethin in there

32mm ✧ f/11 ✧ 1/200   2023

this wasp chased me
around the university of
central florida. I got out of
class and thought yeah
lets be whimsical and take
a picture of these beautiful
creatures against the
brick … yeah … fun . all they
wanted was smoke.

105mm ⋄ f/5.6 ⋄ 1/500   2019

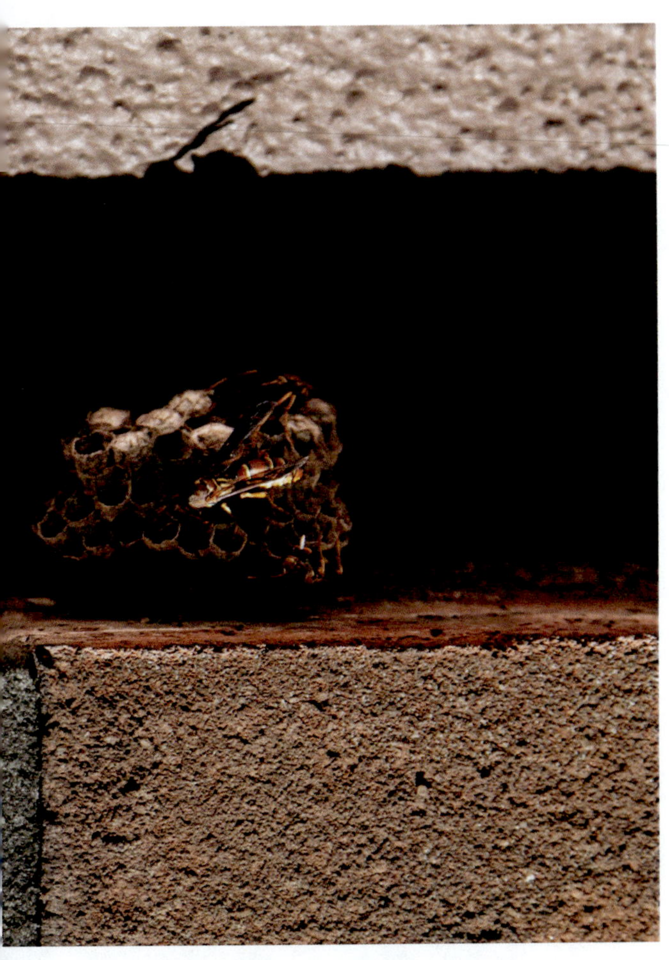

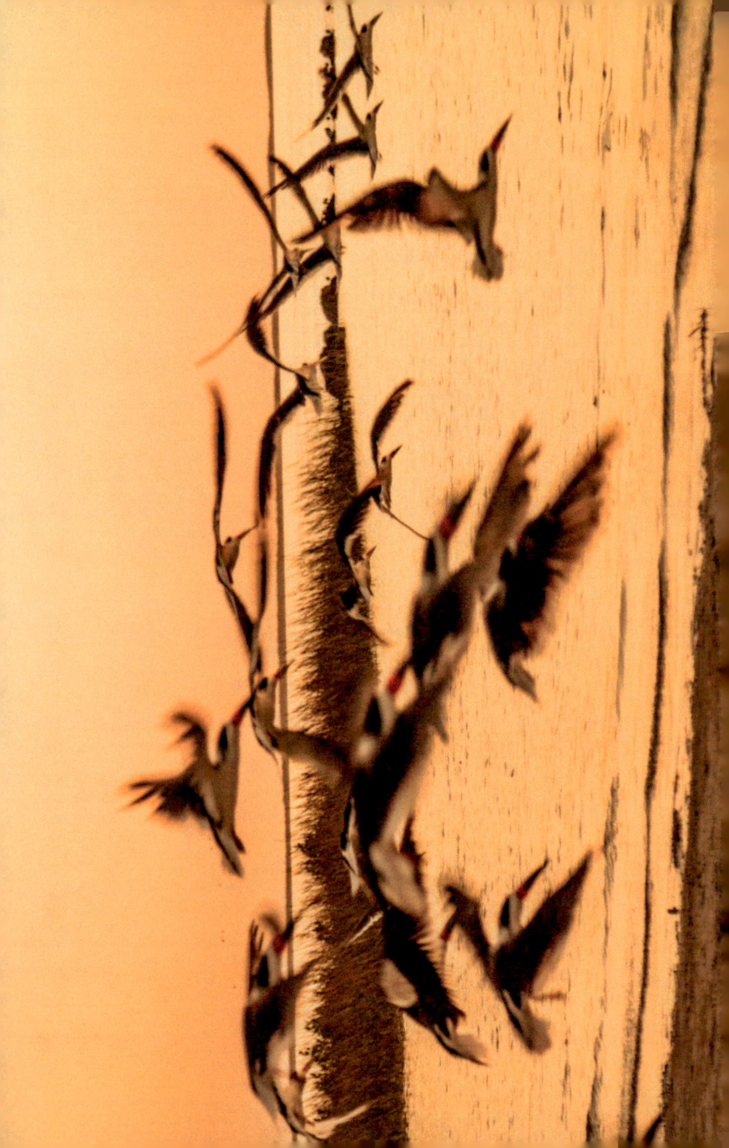

my favorite sunsets are the ones where they knock
out the night sky. BAM, TKO, where it can only
stand after some rest and recovery.

thirty minutes of takeover to exist in a world
ruled by an orange, crimson, passionfruit
colored sky. someone unfamiliar could look
at tampa's water and think it was juice.

85mm ⋄ f/4 ⋄ 1/200   2017

new york, had just got out of a
pizza spot and this fella sees
my camera. he goes "you a
photographer? take my
picture. this some real shit."

i see you unc, you tough

32mm ⋄ f/4 ⋄ 1/100   2021

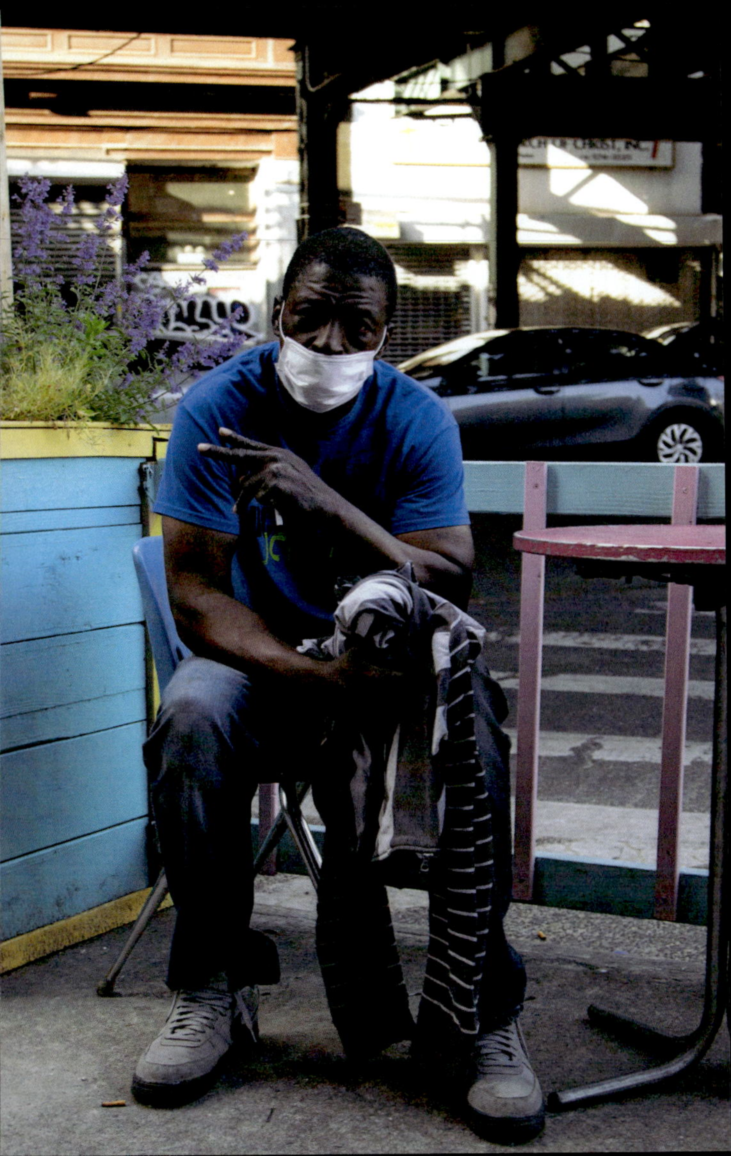

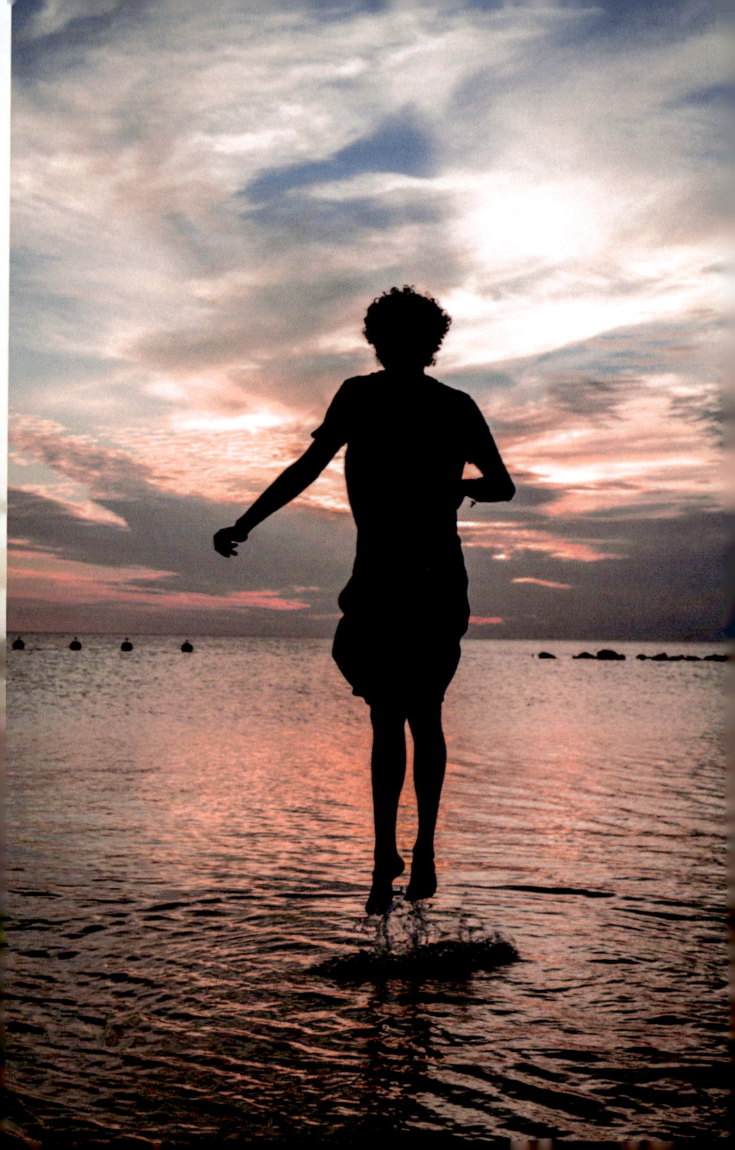

florida water just has a way to
bring some of even the
wildest people together.
warm, calm, and clear — ready
to take the shape of whatever
the sky above it wants.

this memory is marked by
rocky horror, uno, chicken
bake, and a million jumps.

24mm ⋄ f/4 ⋄ 1/250   2018

SX-70 125 ISO square ✧ sonar focused   2025

don't let the blurry calm
film aesthetic fool you,
this memory is viscious.
imagine walking
painstakingly across
many miles, crossing
rocky, dangerous
terrain, searching for a
treaure that simply never
revealed after diligent,
precise, and cunning
wayfinding amidst a
growing desolation
sprouting within.

((we were walking through a park
looking for a four-leaf clover and I
was getting hungry))

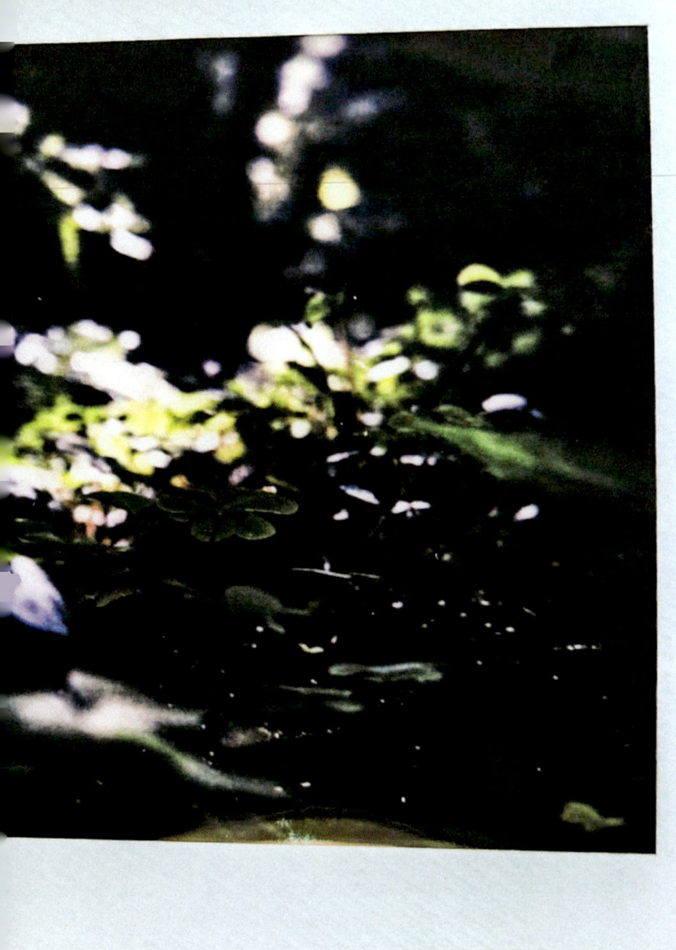

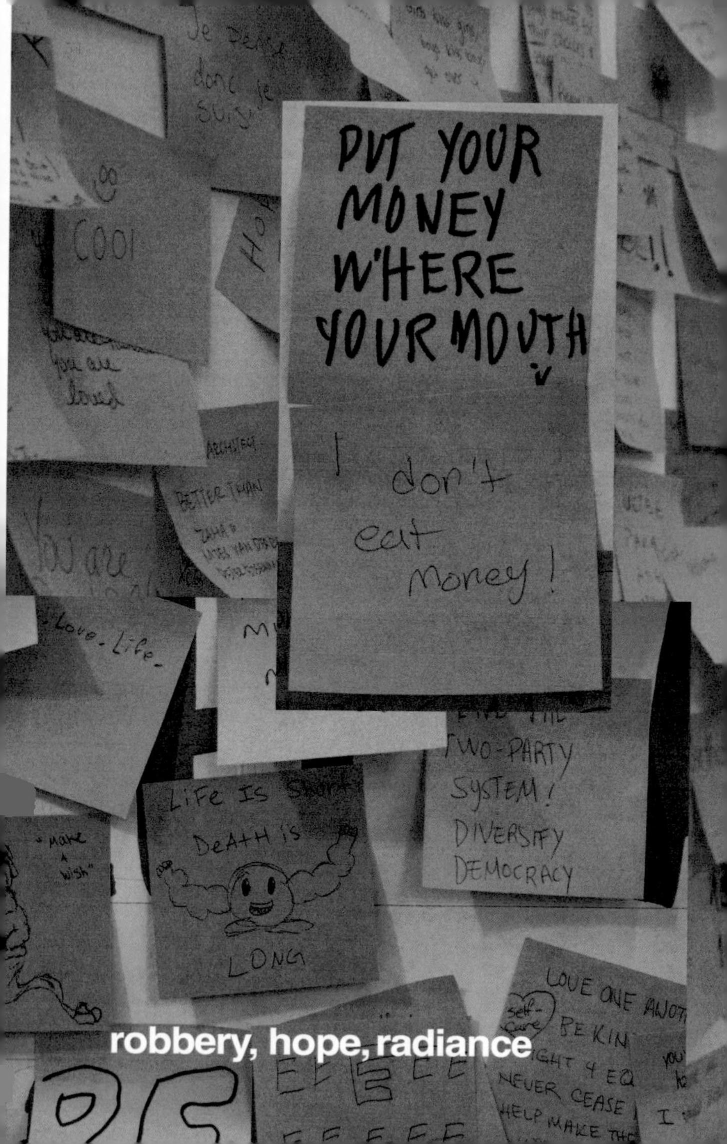
PUT YOUR
MONEY
WHERE
YOUR MOUTH

I don't
eat
money !

COOl

Love-Life-

ARCHITECT
BETTER THAN
ZAHA

"make
a
wish"

Life Is Short
DeAtH is

LONG

TWO-PARTY
SYSTEM !
DIVERSIFY
DEMOCRACY

LOVE ONE ANOT
BE KIN
SELF-
CARE
IGHT 4 EQ
NEVER CEASE
HELP MAKE THE

robbery, hope, radiance

a moment
breath
and just
feel

Don't be afraid
to go for it

PEACE AND LOVE
MY GALAXY

Love
Pe

Chau

Never lose hope of
an ideal future but
Always appreciate the now.

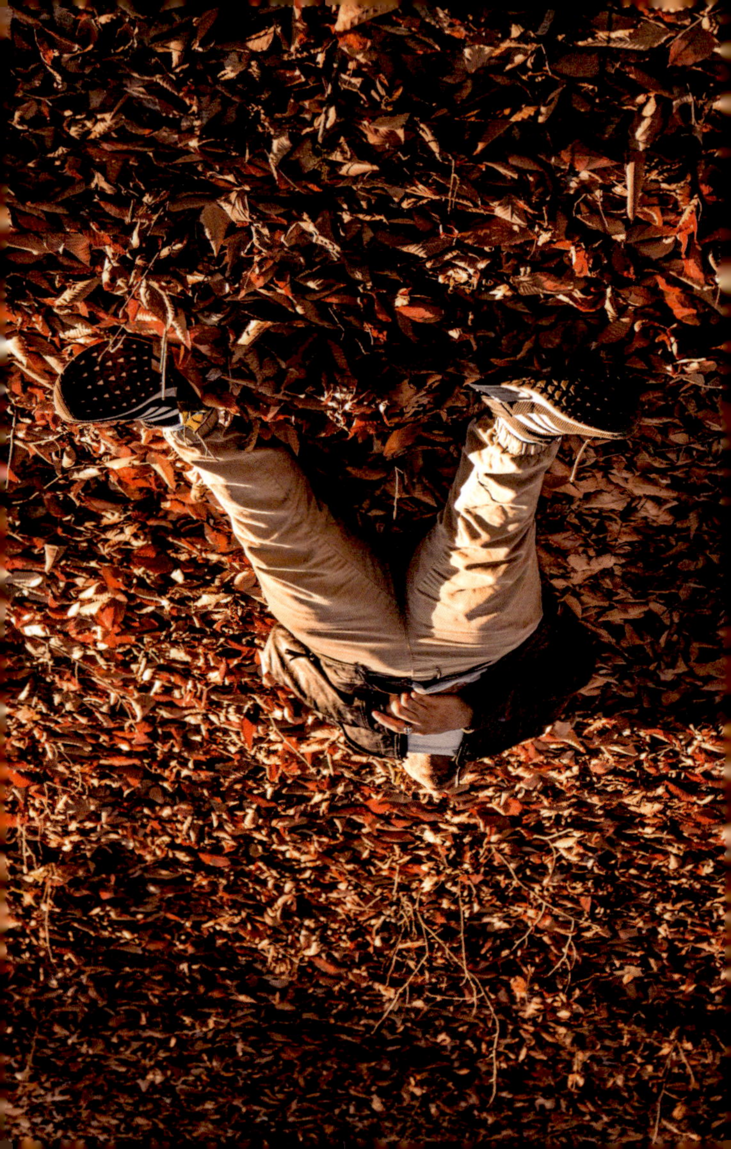

ahh, yes, philly.

on this trip i found a ferret under my butt.

tagging along to see my homeboy's family and origins, i discover this strange, strange land. it was cold, the leaves changed color, and people walked different — the stroll didn't have the aimless swagger i was used to in the south; it was focused and purposeful. we end up in his brother's home and i sit on the couch as they catch up. i feel rumbling, but i thought maybe it was the tacobell from that sixteen hour roadtrip??? i see his lil niece running around, swinging around a long creature that i thought i had only seen in lion king. the rumbling gets worse, and i realize it's the couch beneath me. so out of concern, i disrupt the sibling's conversation to convey what i'm going through. the brother sits down calmly, reaches underneath the cushion i'm sitting on, wiggles his arm a lil bit, and pulls out a full sized meerkat to then place it on my lap. soon thereafter, i learned what a ferret was and reached an understanding for philadelphia.

24mm ✧ f/5.6 ✧ 1/100   2019

nothing like georgia clay after a
rainy day . the canyons reveal
every warm color you could think
of to match the sheer heat and
humidity already huggin ya ,
sprinkled around , you'll find trees
somehow living in the clay ? ? ?
right around the corner you can
get the best wings of your life

24mm ⋄ f/11 ⋄ 1/100   2020

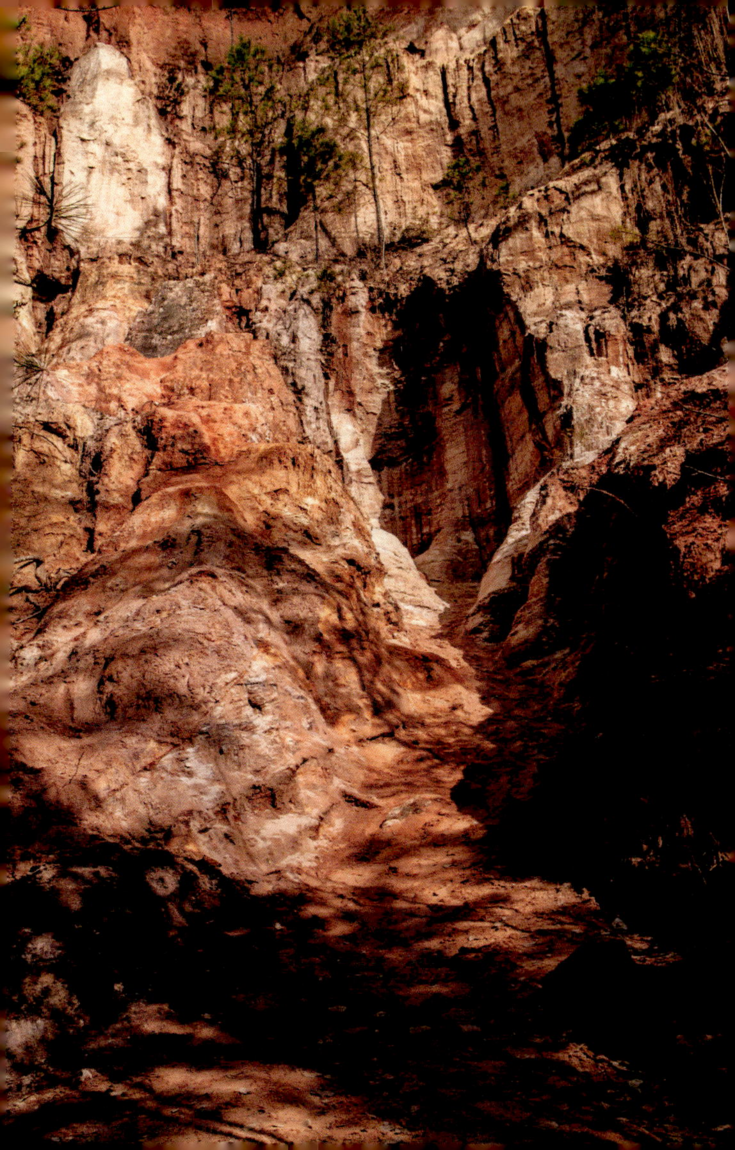

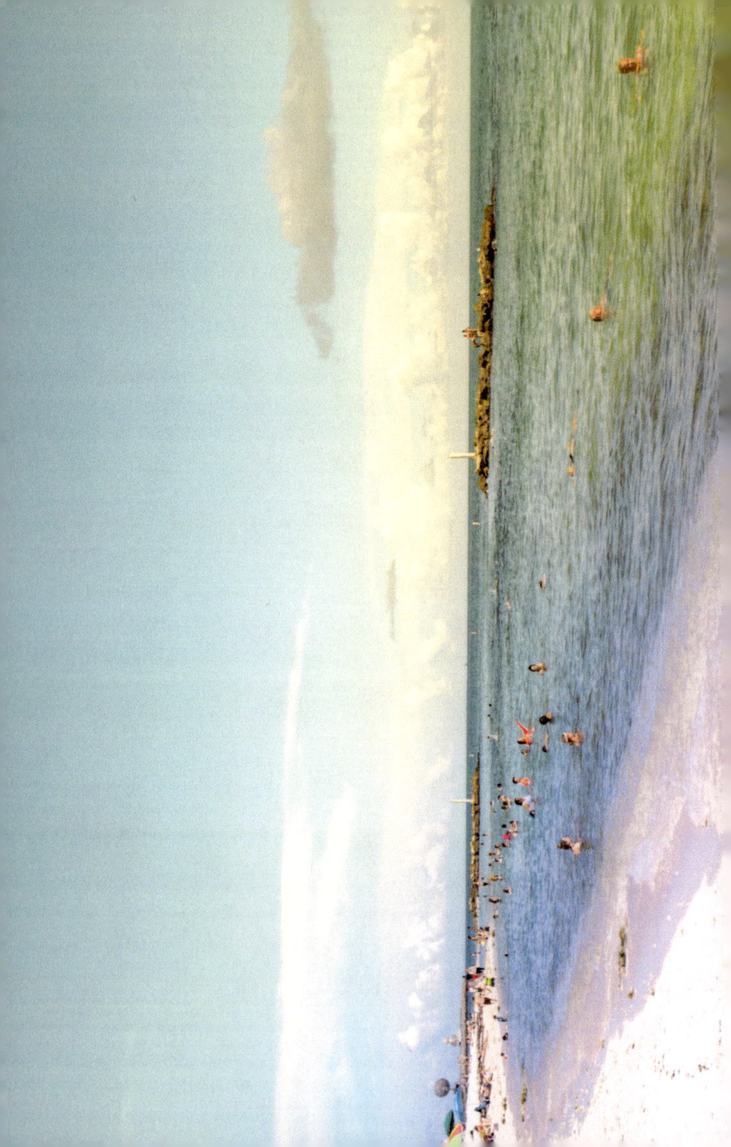

this week was crazy . I had just moved to orlando, got a job at a gas station, got a psychic reading, ended up at the keys, and dropped my camera into the water .

this is just one out of multiple times the ocean's swallowed my camera but this time it actually did something . The auto white balance started tweaking so the color temperatures were off, the lens was no longer removable ??? , it smelled like fire, and it made crackling noises whenever i adjusted the zoom or focus ring . there was also sand in the battery compartment . beautiful day though, and my new friend had a fantastic birthday . the next day i jumped out of an airplane with that fella windows will always be my favorite to photograph. if the light aligns in your favor, you could capture pieces of what's in front of you, behind you, and you yourself — all blended together in a single frame. this one's in a cold brooklyn, where someone got curious about whatever in the world i was lookin at. ma'am i just like reflections

28mm ⋄ f/1.7 ⋄ 1/125   2025

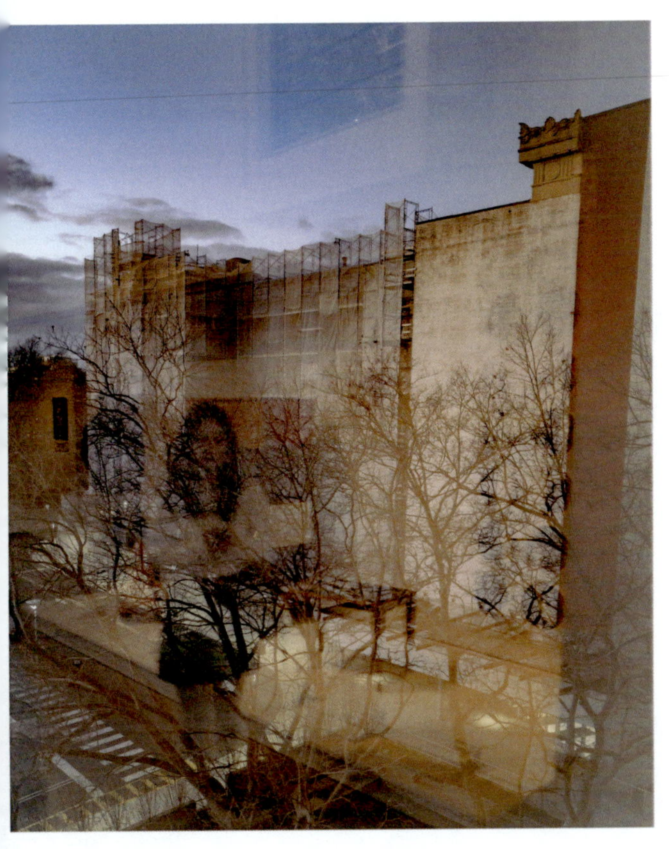

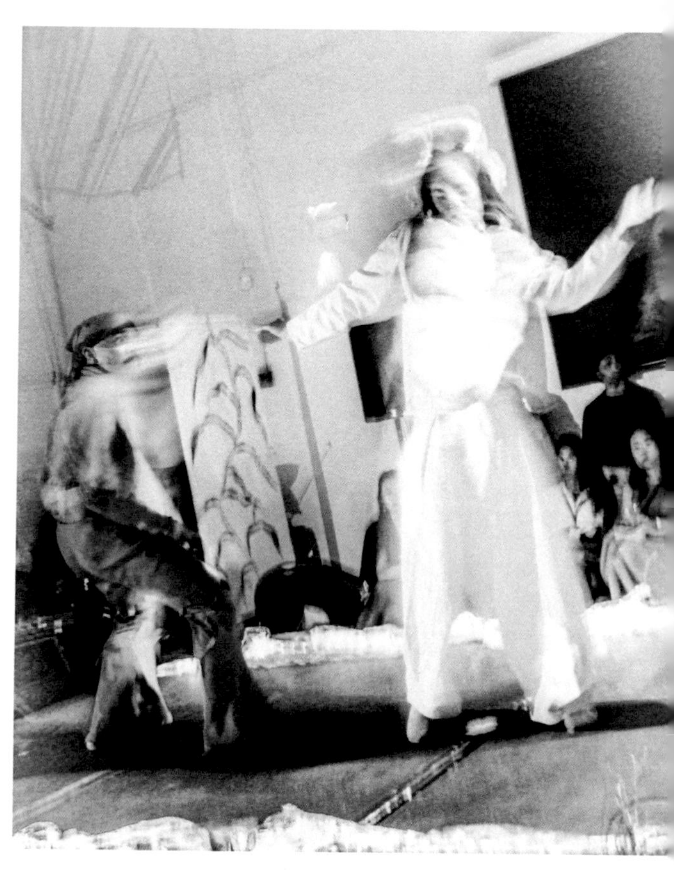

worked with a bay area fashion
show. this thang was straight
up electrifyin. fascinating to
see a story be told through so
many mediums, all under the
span of just about an hour.
each second was filled to the
brim with expression, and it
felt real. everyone was really
there, just doin them.

5mm ◇ f/3.2 ◇ 0.6s   2025

i feel like these donuts would've blessed me.

the light.. blasted from the heavens...

my loved ones restricted me from inspecting further.

28mm ◇ f/6.3 ◇ 1/125   2025

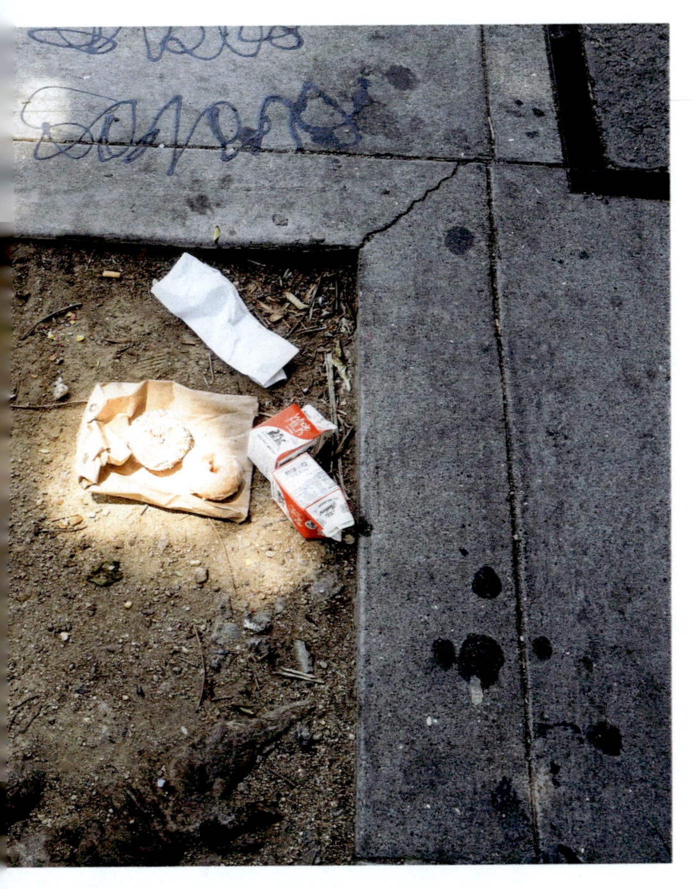

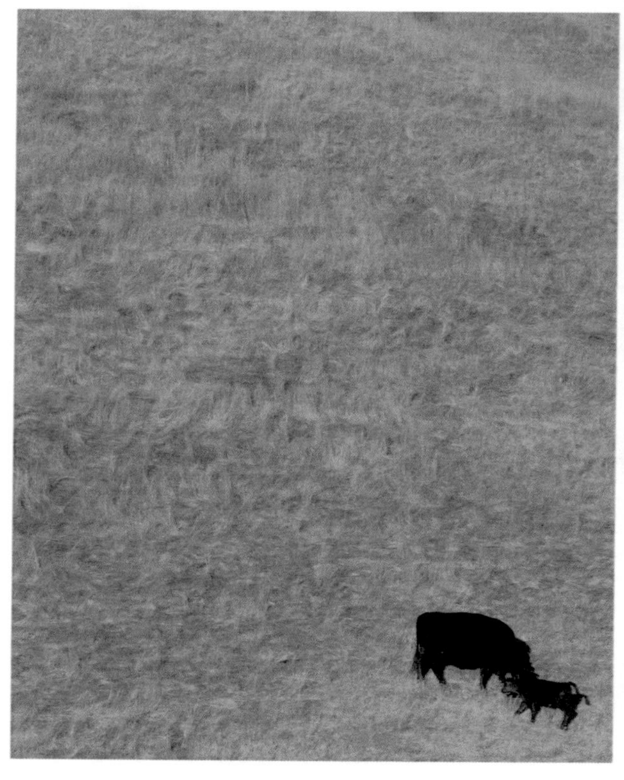

on this day i chased a baby cow with a mexican family.
the sun is setting, i start walking towards the parking lot,
and see an older woman yelling at a bush and waving
her cane. i start walking towards her and whooooosh
there's the cutest little cow running full speed towards
me. i throw my camera over my shoulder and open my
arms, ready for the greatest hug of my life. but the cow
jukes the mess outta me, heading back to the fence.
there i noticed, she accidently jumped out past the
barbed wire but can't jump back in. her mother was goin
MOOOOOOOO on the other side, panicking because
her baby couldn't make it over. realizing the lady with
the cane was trying to help direct the cow towards the
gate, i grew determined. i yell towards her and she
responds back, yelling with the most incoherent
spanish i've ever heard but for whatever reason i
understood. we begin to crowd around the baby, arms
up, cane waving in the air, slowly creepin, then all we
hear is MOOUOOOUUOUUUUU. not from the mother
cow, not from her calf, but from some kid that aparently
is related to the woman with the cane???? this little boy
is running up full speed, the calf is scared, and now
we're all triangulating this cow. another woman
appears, apparently related to them both, starts yelling
angrily at the boy by which the lady with the cane starts
yelling back. i'm using what little spanish i know,
running back and forth across this park now setting by
an orange sky. MOOOOOOOOOOOOO, AQUI AQUI
AQUI, mUoOuOuoUOUo. eventually, another man
arrives and he's able to keep the gate open as we all
chase the baby back to their mother. everyone rejoices,
out of breath, and we all high-five. i still don't really
know what they was sayin

28mm ◇ f/16 ◇ 1/60   2024

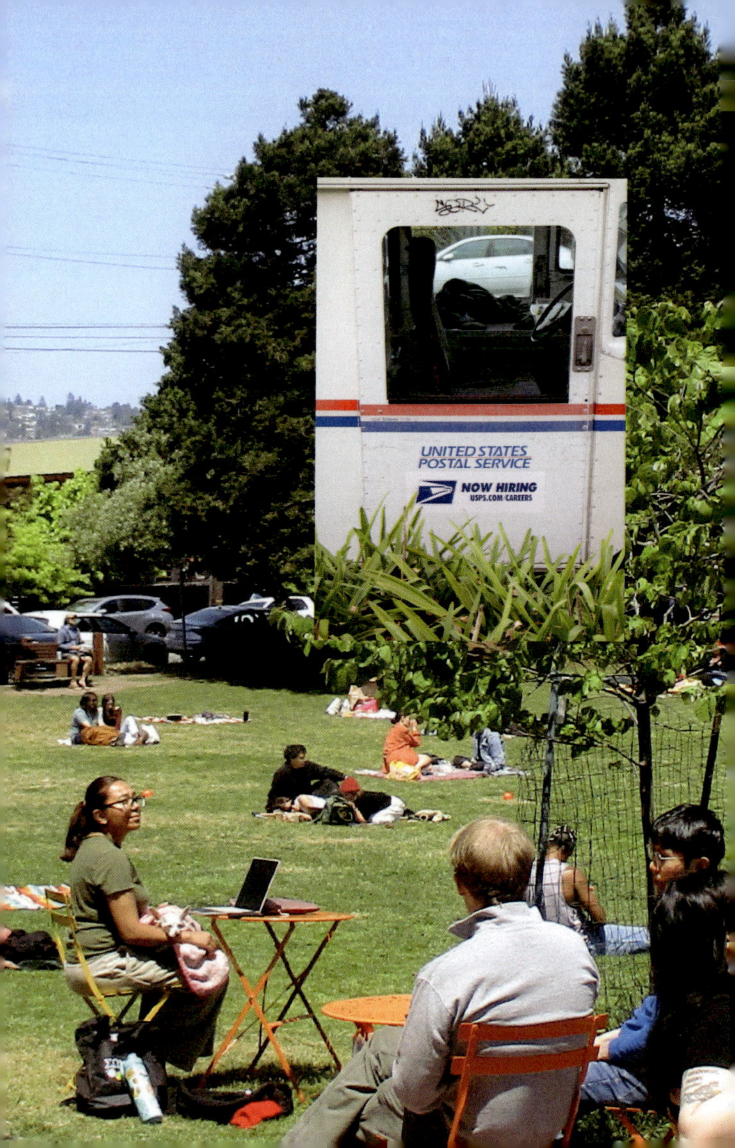

UNITED STATES
POSTAL SERVICE
NOW HIRING
USPS.COM/CAREERS

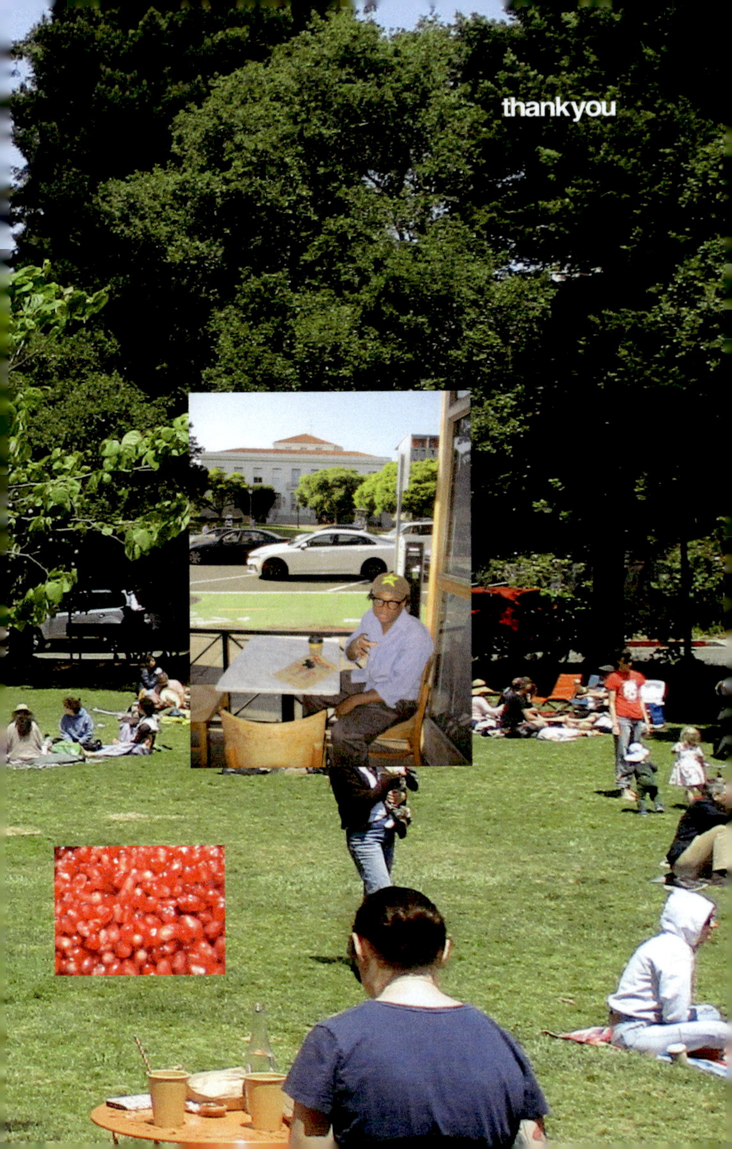

thankyou

little light machines & tools:

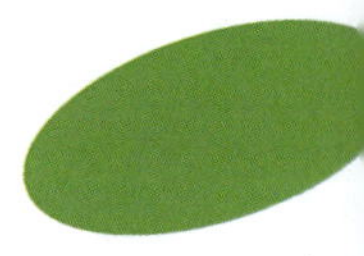

polaroid sx-70

samsung galaxy flip 1

kodak kb10

contax sl300r

canon rebel t3
(this the one that started makin cracklin noises)

lightroom

samsung galaxy s8

canon ae-1

leica q2

www.ingramcontent.com/pod-product-compliance
Lightning Source LLC
Chambersburg PA
CBRC100831110726
48005CB00011B/1049